Empty Space Places You

poems by

Cathy Cain

Finishing Line Press
Georgetown, Kentucky

Empty Space Places You

Copyright © 2018 by Cathy Cain
ISBN 978-1-63534-498-1 First Edition
All rights reserved under International and Pan-American Copyright Conventions. No part of this book may be reproduced in any manner whatsoever without written permission from the publisher, except in the case of brief quotations embodied in critical articles and reviews.

ACKNOWLEDGMENTS

Thank you immensely to Leah Maines, Christen Kincaid, Elizabeth Maines McCleavy and the staff of Finishing Line Press for their collaboration in the publication of this chapbook.

Special thanks to my mentors: David Biespiel, Andrea Hollander, Paulann Petersen and Wendy Willis for reading my work and for their insightful suggestions.

Also thanks to Carl Adamshick, Annie Lighthart, Kim Stafford and to the wonderful community of fellow writers at the Attic Institute of Arts and Letters and the Mountain Writers Series for the profound experience of sharing the world of poetry.

And certainly, heartfelt gratitude to Jennifer Dorner and to my three-year writing group: Tricia Knoll, Carolyn Martin, Pattie Palmer-Baker, and Shawn Aveningo Sanders for their honest feedback, encouragement, and just plain fun.

I am so fortunate and grateful, always, for the sustained support, good cheer, and inspiration of my extended family and dear friends, whom I love so much.

Publisher: Leah Maines
Editor: Christen Kincaid
Cover Art: Cathy Cain
Author Photo: Alex Cain
Cover Design: Elizabeth Maines McCleavy

Printed in the USA on acid-free paper.
Order online: www.finishinglinepress.com
also available on amazon.com

Author inquiries and mail orders:
Finishing Line Press
P. O. Box 1626
Georgetown, Kentucky 40324
U. S. A.

Table of Contents

I Would Buy 1

Navigating the Wind 2

Note to Self: Earthquake Preparedness 4

California Buzz 6

The Miscarriage 7

Landscape 8

Lanterns 10

Philosopher 11

Houseguests 12

Mother with Rabbit, a Memory 13

Watching My Son Do His Physics Homework 14

February Shoes 16

Rogue Weather 2007 17

Believe You Will Walk through the Air 18

Aubade 20

Gravity 22

My Husband's Mother Lies in the Bathtub 24

Cowboy 25

Open Gate 26

Light Switch 27

Kitchen 28

Gather Me 29

Golden Days 30

Snow Goose 31

With love to Dan, Alexander, and Max
In memory of my parents, Vada and Victor

I Would Buy

Pallets of granite, basalt, limestone.
Silos of sand and flying poems.
Crates of candles and stars.

Stock in the sunrise.
Bushels of breeze, bird song,
clouds, blue sky.

Shares in clean air,
pure water, food,
health, comfort, and shelter.

Shipping yards weighted
with living forests, prairies, peace,
and coffee, extra hot.

A cargo plane heavy
with my mother's high heels,
her taffeta slips, her journals, her smile.

Sailing ships full of my father's voice—
all their voices and laughter—
seas of memory.

Trainloads of trust—
my husband's gaze,
steady across the table.

I would buy
vineyards of quiet.
Season tickets to swim through the light.

Navigating the Wind

consider me your doppelganger
made like you of water and air
we are a motion study
a migration
winging through currents
of shared water and air

consider when father
turned a page
in the book of stars
about red shift in dark
then lay back on the carpet
arms and legs stretched out
like spokes of the universe
wheeling   listening to the stars
a usefulness not apparent

or when mother with bare arms and legs
played outside with hose and water
music in sunlit spray
listening to water's touch
on a red rose on cement
on her child's mind
a usefulness not apparent

consider the V of a flock
pulling memory through cirrus clouds
the threads of ghosts around us
then a repositioning of our order
a change in the equation
as I take the lead   fill the migration
with my recollections

consider how a V's wake
wakes a windblown flock
into one weighted dream

the V's discreet undulation
in unison discrete parts
in unison a piercing dart
the wake of a black arrow
funneling beauty

Note to Self: Earthquake Preparedness

Note: There are too many words.

Just make the list.
Note: There will never be enough words.
Note: Start yoga again.

Study the Buddha.
Note: At least learn to spell his name.

Buy some bottled water and a water purifier,
a flashlight, batteries, matches, emergency food.
Cell phones & chargers.
Note: Will they work?

Maybe a bicycle will come in handy.

What will I save?
Shoes and socks. Toilet paper. A jacket.
Flash drives.
Note: Better fill them first.

And business: My ID card.
Note: Also my id.

Immunizations, deeds, accounts, passwords,
family history, my identity.
Note: Which identity?

Best photos—so many.
Note: Make multiples.
Note: There are too many multiples.
Too many of us.
Note: Not enough of us.

Stop the earthquake, the tremors, the torrent in the basement.
Stop climate change. Stop destruction and want.

Note: Too soon it will be our turn.

Quick, get the light.
Note: Strong light in darkness can burn, blind.

Or, the light of kind touch can lead the blind.

Note: What are we who find and lose and find a God?
Note: Mother, Dad, where are you?

Into the night I go with my candle.
Note.

California Buzz

I miss the hum
of golden pollinators, thick
honeybees in yellow acacia,
blossom fuzz dusting

the tree swing's mellow trance,
the Dutch door to the playhouse,
honeysuckle sunned out
against a white fence.

Beyond, the small plot
of orange and lemon trees,
hours, heavy with scent,
low enough to pluck.

Even, under that rock,
the black widow hanging,
red hourglass warning.
You could skirt her with luck.

The Miscarriage

In front of the window, a crystal vase
with yellow roses and shining water,
a gift against gray, lit rain.

I lay alone in the dim room.
He died with me, midterm. My first.
I watched the light-filled petals
drop to the sill without a sound.

Landscape

An elbow, a wrist, this nipple.
My un-pierced earlobe
still small enough to be discreet.
I like this word **still**—as in a quiet presence,
just *still*, as in a landscape uninhabited—
like the landscape of my mother's ashes,
some small sharp-edged shards still there.

I write from the landscape of my body
while I am still here.
Not the first to write from a body, but
the first and only to write from *this* body.
My river hair, my mountain sister breasts,
My fleshy rolling hills and valleys, knobs of finger,
ligament, gristle, and bone.

These bird wrists and thin weak ankles that easily shift,
twist when I step on and roll a pebble,
this shinbone scar from when I fell
onto the edge of the school bus metal step,
this scar on my right thigh where I was pushed
against a gray cinder block,
how its rough edge sliced horizontally,
a bloody gash between tectonic plates
just below the cuff of those pale-blue summer shorts,
just there the ample flesh.
My body is female,
each year having released twelve waiting eggs.
My body broken open for two sons.
From the beginning, their own lands
distinct from mine.

I have loved my toes, short and regular,
though now, they are wrinkled.
Affection for these hands
that wipe the sweat off my brow,

hold the pen or a paring knife,
and for my tongue, my lips—hungry, searching.
My body not forest or desert, nor

a hot city of shimmering glass with reflections
of people walking. Horns honking, motors running,
and written words everywhere—
on the sides of buses and trucks, traffic signs and buildings,
even across people's faces,
words swarming, sliding sideways, down and away
as I walk past each storefront window,

just like they say the great earthquake
will slide the coast range down and away
into the ocean and take with it the Willamette Valley
and me.
Or maybe, my body will be plowed
with the others, like logging debris,
into a huge pile of human corpses burning,

and my ash will drop down through the pyre
and mix with the ash of deer and duck, dogs and cows,
with the ash of volcanoes
erupting along the mountain chain,
even with the ash of my mother.
This life with its terror.
This blessing.

Lanterns

It was just so pretty,
in the old fashioned sense.
We were dining outside at the beach,
watching the slow shadows
shift sand from beige to blue slant,
like a song expanding in counterpoint with the sea.

And there was that other parallel parade,
a serenade among the eucalyptus trees
in lavender and periwinkle light
of small children, unafraid,
walking along the cliff above the sea,
each of them lit by candle shine.
They carried their paper lanterns
bobbing in gentle time.

Philosopher

Life had begun to unfold
in the bold, weighted center above my inner floor.
My second-born sat breech part of his term,
cross-legged, rubbing his hands together
like a wise fool in his garden, rolling dice,
or polishing a charm, smooth in his palms.
He caught touch with a quiet pleasure,
surmised it a metaphysical prize.

Later, while he nursed in my arms, his eyes
held mine. Warm milk intimacy as he lay there,
his arm raised, his finger pointed,
making meanders through the air, as if
playing a line of string, letting out his kite,
discovering time, finding light.

Houseguests

the changing of rooms for the beds
the changing of the beds in the rooms
the changing of people in the beds

of this
what does a child see
who sees the child

to make beds of feather and down
one at a time   with care
white sheets fresh from the laundry line

how they fill and rise with wind   and now
with the flick of my wrist and lace-edged breath
how they billow   then corners tucked in   a pillow fluff

tender   like the craft of Daedalus
father of Icarus
the tip of each wisp

of white feather
embedded into wax
the shape of wing

an arch expanding
wings lifting
rising

our melting
falling
into a sea of night

like a child's soft drop
placed easily
onto a strange bed

Mother with Rabbit, a Memory

She stands in front still,
Mother, holding a bunny.
I did not know she would be so at ease
holding a live bunny near her cheek.

Mother, holding the bunny.
This poem is about light, white light
(she holds the bunny near her cheek),
how light turned through her day.

It's about light, white light,
diffuse, unfolding.
How light turns through the day,
sheen of sheer white,

diffuse, unfolding.
I paint her on canvas, flesh
and blue eyes, on a sheen of sheer white
from the edge of my perception.

I paint in the bunny beside her.
She looks so at ease there,
beyond perception
smiling, standing in front, still.

Watching My Son Do His Physics Homework

Those thick auburn curls, the one that springs free,
drops down, like a poem, always a poem,

to the center of his forehead. He stretches and straightens
his lean, teenage shoulders, resumes his layered thought.

He reads with one bare foot placed
across the top of the other.

I know he possesses energy
by virtue of his position relative to earth.

Gravity both augments his upright stance
and floats, like a buoy, his bright wanderings.

To push a book across a table requires ergs of work.
Work cradles the eye in each of his wings.

When a toddler, he ran by the cat, dangling a long tease.
Ribbons of color now trail from his hand.

Every mass pulls on everything else. The beauty of his face
    keeps me near.
He sees what I do not see, hears the content of my silence.

Like the textbook example, his energy could hit a brick wall,
but his tracks have already been groomed by distant galaxies.

Joules explode in the wake of his work.
In a courtyard bounded by stucco walls, he builds
    a garden of words,

articulated palm fronds dusted in snow, spaces between
pierced with peeks of lemon yellow and peppermint pink.

At dusk, his worded images are complete.

I trust the physics he does, the poetry he thinks.

He handles our large, loping dreams lightly,
coaxing them out of the hushed night.

February Shoes

I'm alone in my studio when
my reflection in the window briefly appears
laid over one dark tree, then turns.
That's when I remember my mother walking away,
her high heels reflected on a cold polished floor.

Through my shape in the window, I see her
retreat again—now into a landscape, that one dark tree
nearer than the others, stark against the white of winter.
Three blackbirds sit on an empty branch.
Below are a child's shoe prints, blue in the snow,
a child who has wandered away—

My mother as that child. Alone
in a white wool coat,
blue hat, and long blue scarf.
A child who has fallen in the snow,
arms and legs askew, awkward with ache,
her body like an inverted chair.
She rises, lifts her delicate, pointy elbows,
a child in flight, like a blown snowflake.

I see it all there, the years of her life,
her shoes repeated
through a walk of time—

shoes placed neatly in horizontal lines,
the backs of her many high heels
arranged on shelves in her closet's theater,
like spectators watching, in tiers,
as blackbirds fly out of sight,
and a child in snowy white disappears.

Rogue Weather 2007
—*for my son, Alexander*

On the porch, when I had released my hold,
        you held me close, held me hard.

You leaned away from me,
        hooked your body into the wind, and were gone.

The storm's wail like a train that had gained on us,
        like my moan at your birth—
        enough to bring us both down
        if I did not let you face the wind alone.

My love for you like that storm—
        enough to sweep miles of air across the land,
        enough to topple century-old trees,
        lay them, massive, across branch-covered roads,
        split houses wide.

My voice *Don't go!* rising with the roar
        as I reached out, all raw within,
        and followed when you went
        for your winter jacket,
        your gloves, your favorite blue hat.

Our world cracking. The scent of ozone.
        Your drive to breathe separately—
        as if that scent had billowed your lungs,
        blown us apart,
        allowed you to fly into your life.

Oh, that ozone. Oh, my son.

You had never been in such a storm.

How the leaves, one at a time, began to unsettle,
the stillness before it began.

Believe You Will Walk through the Air
—for my son, Max

When you were a small child,
you rose up slowly
out of your frightened squat
behind the couch.
You peeked with one eye over the top
at the tightrope walker
on the screen across the room.

You already understood
the possible consequence
of what you saw.

~

And now, love has reacquainted you
with fear.

~

Remember that walker?
His horizontal pole,
the long bar tilting slightly,
one end down, then the other,
lovely subtle dips,
the welcome ease
of his holding,
palms turned up?

The braided cable
on which he walked
had strands that spiraled
round each other,
a vine tendril growing,
propelling him through the air.

~

Slip on the elk skin shoe
I made for you,
formed exactly to your arch.
Let me wrap and rewrap
your under sole.

Do you sense the silence at your core,
your chest a taut whisper,
the weight of your own offered palms
outstretched in the air—
your ballast pole
like a line extending
across a butterfly's wing
that dips as it opens
and rises to close?

Empty space places you
there, and there.
Feel the welcome ease
of its holding.

~

Exhale your self.
Curl your instep
over that exquisite edge,
the hollow of your soul
meant for this.

Now with your eyes, reach.

Aubade
—for my grandson, Auden

How far you have traveled, swaying
in dewy slumber, a slow roll through night.

Ladies and gentlemen, we have begun our descent…
Secure your belongings for landing.
Fasten your seat belt.

My plane jolts like your head pushing your
mother's pelvic floor. Your father reminded
me these bold shocks are merely waves riding
an ocean of air. I will not sink. Nor
will you—our hard-set resolution bumping
against roaring night's red-banded door.

Through dove-gray thoughts, each ferried dreamer
is caught mid-gesture—yesterday's newspaper held
at an impossible angle, a jostled stir,
a sharp head nod, an arm jerked to alert
before settling down—like birds,
small adjustments in a flock, assured.

Your eyes not yet ready to share their dark pools of song—
your brows furrow away the coming light,
too bright, after that world of muted color
and shaman sound. We will wait for your words.
Your finger to your cheek now, quiet, pensive,
pondering whether you wish to endure

door slams, bell rings, and abruptly dropped books,
not sure, even, of melodic cooings,
or eventual intricacies like
blintzes, coffee, and cell phone welcomings.
Janus-faced in this liminal place, you turn
one side back towards conception's moonrise,

the other to persimmon sunrise
and love's grace.

You startle as you enter dawn's portal.
Last eve's rocky ride, unclear if you would
thrive, but you do. New child arriving,
hold on to yourself as you become mortal.

The clank of landing gear seems almost too late.
Jet brakes screech like the parrots, jade green,
in play above Buena Vista's sunlit trees.
God's wind funnels you into morning.
With our unspoken connection, you come
to stay, a full stop in the light of day.

We are at the gate.

Gravity

A-tisket a-tasket
A green and yellow basket.

We tuck the basket away,
the one brimming with my collection of pool balls,
hide it behind the cozy, overstuffed chair
in the corner of the family room
where our home sits small in the forest
among towering conifers.
We hide it to protect our two-year old grandson
and our old oak floor.
Polished pool balls, vivid,
like our love letters through the years.

A fluttering love letter is not a hefty pool ball, and yet...
both contain a sound of chaos boldly colored.

~

I wrote a letter to my love,
And on the way I dropped it,

We should have known all that color would call him,
that he'd find the basket.

I show him the difference
between *drop* and *set*—
between *throw* and *roll*—
a question of touch,
a moment's more holding.

He begins to learn the pros and cons of gravity,
the weight of relationship—
sets a ball down and rolls it, looks sideways at me,
launches another across the floor,
hears the double pitch, the chain reaction,

as one ball knocks against the next.
He practices rolling them faster and faster,
squeals with delight.
Flashes of red, blue, orange, green,

and yellow, until he loses control,
sends them several at once, a great thundering and clacking—
like a bowling match among the gods,
like the Big Bang Theory,
like our love.

~

And on the way…

Love letters
dropped through the years,
flashes of red, blue, orange, green, and yellow.
The child watching—
as our bright memories roll gaily
down shadowed hills,
over the moist and bumpy softness of the forest floor
and our dark fallings among the trees.

My Husband's Mother Lies in the Bathtub

the tree falls with a boom
shakes the ground
indents soft earth
she weighs so little so little

there is nothing left
to save or ship
paper bills all around
a white fluttering fluttering

the bed sheets and mattress
have been ripped apart
the neighbors stand back
watching and watching

what to do what to do
I am calling calling

Cowboy

The dull finish of that old pale-apricot pickup,
the one my mother's lover owned,
fades into the desert.
The smell of new leather long gone—
instead, a shredded, dusty-stuffing scent.

He embroidered one tale after another—
how he rode in the ice-delivery truck,
how he and his three brothers
cooked up wild havoc in Perris, California—
how he walked for hours across dry,
open hills to survey the land,
tended his persimmon and avocado trees,
wrestled sprinkler heads and rattlesnakes,
and always wore those pressed levis
that he himself had ironed in the garage.
How, in black cowboy hat and boots, he danced
with my widowed mother into the long night.

He stared down his death horse for days,
drinking only water. His whispered rasp,
Yuck, tastes like warm horse pee!

Where's my gravy and biscuits?
I ordered three dozen!
Will you miss me at dinner?

His strong, rugged shape shrunk
like thin rust and desert bone,
and yet, he wanted to drive
that old truck back home.

Open Gate

Shot upright by a morphine jolt,
fear in her blue eyes, she steels herself
for the next unfolding surprise.
Like Lot's wife, she glances back.

Later, her head rests heavy on my chest,
until her last labored breath unties us.
Now, her upturned face reflects soft lamplight
with a beauty beyond me this cold night.

Her back fever-hot with sweat
from leaving us and all she knew,
her spirit loosens like the rising moon.
Erase our safe embrace. Take her.

Open these windows, doors, and latched gates.
Let the moonlight of my mother's face pervade.

Light Switch

Like God, she
quietly turns off
the light above
the sleeping
infant bud.

Sleep my winged child.
Paint yourself slowly
into the pure light of night.
Alone you will proceed
into your picture,
Alone. You will be alone.

Kitchen
—for Mother

Death came unwelcome as an unseen rat
to snatch away your hot, delicious health.
Fierce loss of saucy self, of every breath,
a tale in disbelief and dolor writ.

I numbered each item of inner wealth
in my kitchen, tried to make ingredients fit.
Each recipe fell flat.
I could not zest your death.

Yet, your last keen breath
was reverent, with instruction writ
to clear my palate from grief's funk, that rat.
You left me with an appetite for health.

Your ash on my finger could never taste flat.
Into numbness, I now scatter your death
like lemon rind, shake out your spicy wealth.
Your life in mine, a rich and piquant fit.

Gather Me

> *Come, come, whoever you are . . . Ours is not a caravan of despair.*
> —Rumi
> *I am always not what I am and I am always what I am not.*
> —Nam June Paik

I'm lost on the clean line that came before and continues to lead.
I trace it here, along the painted river,
how it defines the highlight of a ripple, then flows to the bank,
to lush low willows, follows the trunk of an overhanging birch,
and out along a branch, out to the smallest twig and leaf—

Now it skips to the mountain ridge, edges the horizon,
then jumps back to my vision of you—
marks an eyelash resting on your cheek, the edge
    of skin above your nostril,
the outline of all your contours   a squiggle, scribbled as you turn—

you, the singular   you, the plural
the reader   the viewer of the river in my painting
you, in sunlight tasting a strawberry, cool red juice
    at the corner of your lips
you, the one I'm in love with   the one I don't know
the one with sparkling laughter   you, with hurt
    hidden behind your pocket
you, who hold a pen   you, the one who plays the paintbrush
the one that speaks of others' confusion   you, confused
you, my sister   my daughter not born   my sons
    my lover, my husband
you, the river that catches aqua paint from the sky
you, who hold me   you, whom I hold after the storm
you, who stop me when I look in the mirror   you, who haunt me
you, smelling of new cut grass, summer sap rising
    warm under rough bark
you, who touch my palm
you, who turn toward me   then turn away
you, the Maker of flesh and contour line—

Gather me in your arms, in your arms.
Never to emigrate, never to leave—
give me more time.

Golden Days

Weaving simple
Maypole patterns,
children skip
unknowingly
into more
complicated
being.

Snow Goose

Grandma, do you have my Goosey book?
Yes, I do. I do. I will bring it
up from the basement box
and read it now to you.

Will you read me my basement book,
the one I made last time?
Yes, I will, I will, my love.
I will read it one more time.

Title with wonder these books you make,
these books that house your dreams.
Be brave, be brave, my little goose.
Sweep the white sky with your wings.

Your gathered rhymes and silly tales
will flow like clouds around the moon.
Color your pictures, my little goose.
Sweep up stories as if with a broom.

Tonight, the snow is falling, falling—
snowflakes that make us sing
of white goose feathers, and smiling stars,
and the fairy dust Grandma brings.

Come sit in my lap in your cloud pajamas.
Use your broom to stave off the cold.
As we read your stories, my love, my love,
I'll forget that I grow old.

Come, sweep me into your Goosey book,
this one I help you hold.
Sweep me up with the sparkling dust,
the clouds of icy snow.

Cathy Cain's work received the Kay Snow 2016 Paulann Petersen Poetry Award from Willamette Writers; the 2015 Edwin Markham Prize for Poetry from *Reed Magazine*; and recognition from the Oregon Poetry Association. Her poetry has appeared in *VoiceCatcher, Reed Magazine, The Poeming Pigeon,* and is forthcoming in *Verseweavers*. Cathy has served as a poetry co-editor at *VoiceCatcher*. She is a two-year Poet's Studio alumna and a 2014-2015 Atheneum Fellow, both at the Attic Institute, Portland, Oregon. Additionally, she has studied with Portland's Mountain Writers. Cathy holds degrees in literature and visual art from Lewis & Clark College, MAT; Oregon State University, BFA; and University of Washington, BA, Phi Beta Kappa. Cathy is also a painter and printmaker. She taught in the public schools for over thirty years. Cathy lives with her husband near Portland, Oregon.

www.ingramcontent.com/pod-product-compliance
Lightning Source LLC
LaVergne TN
LVHW051529070426
835507LV00023B/3381